Losing Mom

a family's journey of transition, hope & perseverance

Frances Wollman Baumgarten Ph.D

ISBN: 1460928091
ISBN 13: 9781460928097

Acknowledgments

I would like to express my deepest gratitude to all of the children, teens, parents, and families who have allowed me to be part of their cancer journey. Their courage and determination to help and support each other is breathtaking; it has truly been an honor to be included in their lives.

To the Board of Directors at the Center for Cancer Counseling, this novel would not have been possible without your continued support and tireless effort to our mission of being able to offer therapeutic services to every family dealing with cancer. Together, we have accomplished our goal of ensuring that any family dealing with cancer is not alone with their pain and struggles, and has a safe place to develop strong coping skills and strategies.

To the physicians and physician assistants, who entrust us with their patients, and the nurses, social workers, and therapists, who use the Center as a resource, thank you.

To the donors, whose dedication to the Center has enabled us to provide much needed services to our cancer patients, and their family members, we extend our appreciation and a heartfelt thank you.

A special thanks to those who assisted in editing and ensuring that this novel was polished: Joanne Ramirez for a beautiful front and back cover design, and her continued ability to capture the essence and emotion of our work at the Center; Joanne Reynolds for her interest and smart editing suggestions and willingness to help whenever asked; Jeff Perlman for offering his expertise in editing.

To my colleague and dearest friend Dr. George Orras, my deepest gratitude for co-founding and making the dream of the Center come to fruition.

A forever grateful thank you to Dr. Neil Barth whose compassionate and aggressive medical treatments afforded me a rich and fulfilling life, and for his warm persistent encouragement which started me down this specialized therapeutic path.

To my family: My darling husband Joel, daughters Helen and Hani, mothers Shirley and Charlotte, and dear sister Marna, for reading, rereading, and offering endless hours of guidance and feedback, Aunt Sonia whose finishing touches helped wrap up this novel; and Judi Hoelderlin for her thoughtful comments, and a lifetime of friendship. Words cannot express how much I value all of your opinions and suggestions, or how grateful I am for your love and support.

Introduction

Losing Mom is a heartfelt novel that originated from my years of working with children, teens, and young adults, as well as parents, during a parent's diagnosis, treatment, and death from cancer.

Losing Mom is my opportunity to give voice to their thoughts, struggles, and emotions, so that you, the adult in their life, can truly understand what this experience feels like and how it impacts their entire lives.

Children and teens are notorious for not sharing information when a parent is ill. When I ask the children, "Do you talk to anyone about your feelings?" They say, "No." When they tell me how they cry themselves to sleep at night, I ask, "Do you go to your mom or dad (the well or surviving parent) for help?" They often reply, "I don't want to be a burden." Their memories are always ambivalent. Good memories are now filled with pain and loss; memories of their misbehavior now sport tons of guilt and sorrow. Managing these emotions is an enormous challenge that most adults struggle with, let alone a child who has fewer resources.

This novel is a chronicle of Stella, from ages eight through twenty-one, and her four siblings as they deal with their mother's illness and death from cancer, the developmental challenges of growing up without a mom, the discussions and insights they share as they grow older and are better able to communicate and express their feelings about their loss, and their mother's final message to them. The experiences that Stella and her siblings talk about are real and have been told to me hundreds of times.

Children, teens, and young adults experience the illness and death of a parent in similar ways. Their needs during this time are consistent, their grief runs a familiar pattern, and their life takes on a very different flavor than it once was.

The illness and loss of a parent is a life-altering experience, which sends children and teens into years of a roller coaster-like grief cycle. Just because our children are silent—in word and behavior — about their emotions of sadness, loss, and grief, this silence does not negate the devastating and life-altering ways that they are affected. It is not uncommon for children to look like they are functioning well. This silence fools everyone, at least for some time. Eventually, their grief spills over, as if out of the blue, leaving the adults befuddled, confused, and usually unable to connect the dots.

As adults, we are at a terrible disadvantage in understanding what this experience is like for them. At a time when these children need us the most, we are lost as to how to help. In addition, the surviving parent, siblings, relatives, and friends are dealing with their own grief and sorrow.

It is only through the hours upon hours with these children, teens, and young adults, that I have developed an appreciation and understanding of how they think, cope, and deal with their parent's illness and death. In deciding how best to share this information, how best to educate the adult world about this experience, I decided that taking you through *their* journey, in this novel, is by far the best illustration. Merely writing another self-help book would not do justice to the children and their experience. With as much empathy or sympathy as we can possibly imagine, living in someone else's shoes and feeling their feelings is a much stronger and truer experience than hearing explanations.

As painful as this journey is, it is filled with hope, helpful hints, things to watch out for, suggestions for coping, and a deep insight into growing up under extraordinary life circumstances.

Sincerely,

Frances Wollman Baumgarten, Ph.D.
"Center for Cancer Counseling"

Well…I didn't actually lose my mom…not like in can't find and can't remember where I put her. My mom died. Our journey started a long time ago… when I was just a baby, just eight-years-old. Now that I am all grown up at thirteen, graduating junior high and going on to high school, I am ready to share our tale…my writings…my thoughts.

Age Eight

The Beginning

After a fairly ordinary day at school, I came home to find a great surprise. Momma was in the kitchen baking cookies. What a treat, Momma was usually at work in the afternoon. After we talked, kissed, and hugged, she said that she had something to tell me. She said that she had been busy today and found out that she had something called cancer. Now, I didn't know if this was an animal—maybe we had a new puppy or kitten. But no, cancer was an illness, she explained, and she needed to take special medicine to get better. I couldn't understand what the big deal was. After all, we had all taken turns being sick, and the best part was staying home and watching movies all day. She explained that this was a bit different and that the medicine would make her tired and her hair would be falling out. "What kind of medicine makes your hair fall out? I sure don't ever want to take that by mistake," I said. She hugged and kissed me and told me she would make sure I didn't get her medicine by mistake. Now, I know mistakes happen, and so do accidents. So for a long time, just to make sure, I double-checked all of my food and drinks.

Momma always told us the truth and the importance of never lying. Yet Momma had a weird look in her eyes. When I asked her if she was scared, she told me, "Absolutely not! Everything is going to be just fine." I heard the words and saw her eyes, and now I was scared. Why would Momma tell me something she didn't believe? You know I can't call her a liar—that is rude and disrespectful. But I know that look. That look was telling me that I needed to do something. The question is what? What do you do when your momma needs some big time, serious, extra help? If I can come up with a good plan, I think I can be that extra help and the one to save Momma.

So here it is. My plan is to be just like Superman and have a secret identity. In the daytime, I will be like Clark Kent, a journalist, and then by nightfall, my superpowers will kick in. At nighttime, I will pray and pray, knowing that my super energy will help Momma get better. By daylight, I will be the future journalist of the family (definitely the best way for me to disguise my real mission of saving Momma).

To start I must tell you that Momma is very smart…in fact our entire family is. There are six of us: Momma, me (I am the baby of the family), Elizabeth is twenty-five, William is twenty-three, Rosalind is twenty-one, and Paul is fifteen. My name is Stella, and I'm eight. All of us kids are named after early Hollywood movie star greats: Elizabeth Taylor, William Holden, Rosalind Russell, Paul Newman, and me, I'm named after a movie character Stella Dallas. Momma always says this is for my drama skills and love of jewelry. What is with the movie star names you ask? Momma says this is because, in her heart of hearts, she knew that we'd have plenty of brainpower— but, maybe, just maybe, we'd need a little bit of extra glitz. Where is our dad you ask? Good question. He left a long time ago, so I no longer count him as part of our family. The advantage of being the baby of the family is that you have plenty of adult people to boss you around, so you don't miss another one. I think my family is pretty special; all six of us live together, spend a lot of time together, and have wonderful adventures. In addition to my family, we have many aunts, uncles, cousins, and grandparents to make plenty of noise and messes on the holidays. We're talking about a lot of people at family parties (which are always tons of fun).

Getting back to the task on hand, I have decided that the best way to tell my tale is to interview my family. Everyone always tells me how creative I am, and, after all, I am now the official family journalist. So, interviewing my family seems like the best way to record our lives. This is actually OUR story… my sisters and brothers, me, and, of course, our mom.

As my teacher always says, a good story has a beginning, middle, and end. I think my family thought this was a cute project—the perfect thing to keep me occupied and out of their hair.

Little did they know what these interviews would be like. Little did they know that my writing would document the years leading up to our mother's death.

I really wanted to start with Momma since she was the beginning, but I fudged a bit and started with Elizabeth. I figured she was old enough to know most of the good stuff about the family.

Elizabeth, as I said, is the oldest. She is beautiful, smart, and talented. As far back as I can remember, Elizabeth has been like my second mom. Always there, always interested, and always involved. When I was little, I think I was like her toy. She'd take me shopping, dress me up, do my nails, and experiment on me with new makeup styles. She still takes me shopping and does my nails, but now it is for me. At night, when I would be lonely or scared, it was Elizabeth's bed that I climbed into, and still do. She is always available with a hug and kiss. Out of all my siblings, she is the only one who is never annoyed with me, no matter how difficult I am. She is also a creative writer. After graduating from college, Elizabeth got a job with the local newspaper. She is in charge of writing what they call their human-interest stories. These are stories like mine, about people and things happening in the community. I guess she is the reason that I like to write. What I wanted from Elizabeth were her memories.

She started her story by showing me pictures of her, Momma, and you guessed, Dad. The people in the pictures looked so happy holding this little baby.

Elizabeth: Oh, Stella, look how young and beautiful Momma is in this picture, just twenty-one, the same age Rosalind is now. Because Dad and Mom were still in college, we lived with Nana and Poppa (Momma's parents), so that they could help take care of me. It was so nice having the entire family living in the neighborhood. There was always somebody in and out of the house and always somebody to play with. When I was two-years-old, we moved into our own apartment. Dad was working, and Momma had just finished her education when she found herself pregnant again. I will never forget when they brought William home from the hospital. All he did was cry and all I wanted was to be at Nana and Poppa's. Fortunately, I started school and fell in love. I always loved being at school; reading and writing were my favorite subjects. School was definitely my escape. There really isn't too much to tell except that Momma kept having babies, and the house was always busy and hectic. But when you were born, Stella, something changed. You were so special; I felt like you were mine. Dad left just before you were born. It was a shock to all of us because Mom and Dad never fought or argued. Dad was never around much, always working, getting home late, and leaving early. He worked on Saturdays, and although he was home on Sundays, he was usually occupied with one project or another. As kids, we didn't pay much attention to Dad's absence or his lack of participation in the family. Also, at this point, we were living in this house, never venturing far from Nana and Poppa, and the extended family. It is as if Momma instinctively knew we needed to be surrounded by them. There were so many relatives in and out of the house, and life was so busy with school, activities, and helping Momma, that there really wasn't time to think about anything else.

All of a sudden, right smack in the middle of my sister talking, my great idea started to feel like a terrible idea. I didn't want to hear all of this. I didn't ask about Dad. I thought I'd get funny stories to laugh about.

Elizabeth: I guess, Stella, my story may be a bit colored by Momma's illness. Since we were always a team, I never considered what would happen if Mom were ill and really needed me to take care of the family.

Well, I had about enough of this mush. I told Elizabeth thank you, but it was time for me to gather info from the others. After a big hug and kiss, I ran off as fast as I could.

William, being the second oldest, was my next target and definitely not as easy to capture. William is the busiest and probably the smartest of us all. He is a scientist and is determined to make some breakthrough medical research discovery. He works long hours in the lab, but always manages to be home on Sunday to just hang out. He likes to cook and usually makes Sunday dinner. He always has something interesting to talk about. Sometimes, for a special treat, he takes me to the lab and we examine cells under the microscope.

William started his story by saying that he thinks I am absolutely adorable. I know this is true because he always calls me cutie pie and taps me on the head. He said I am the great distraction of the family, always talking and asking questions.

As he continued, William didn't have too much to say about his history. His tales were about Nana and Poppa playing cards with him and buying him his first microscope—dissecting worms as a kid—and always having frogeyes or some other disgusting experiment happening.

Since William shares a room with Paul, he had to move his miniature lab to Nana and Poppa's and ended up spending most of his time there.

Luckily, William didn't get all sappy with me. He said that he is trying to be home more, now that Momma is sick. And since he is the science guy, he is the best one to help Momma with the medical stuff—taking her to doctor's appointments and learning all about her illness and treatments. Like I said, we are a tight family, always there for one another. When I asked him "Are you scared?" He said, "No. There is really no reason to be scared. The doctor is very smart, just like all of us, and he has magic for Momma."

Well…magic…OK, that is fine, but I know that it will be my superpower that gets us through this. After all, everyone in the family seems to have a role in helping Momma; I'm excited that mine is the secret one.

Now let's not forget, William was talking to an eight-year-old he called cutie pie. Now at thirteen, I can see he was trying to protect me.

Rosalind is also always busy, but not too busy for me. She is in her fourth year of college, getting ready to graduate and go onto another school, they call graduate school. Rosalind is going to be an astronaut. She is my hero. She wants to be the first woman to explore Mars. I don't understand why everyone, except Momma, says she is the dreamer of the family. Momma always tells us that we can do whatever we set our minds to. Rosalind is out to prove her right.

Since Momma is so busy at doctor appointments or just not feeling well, Rosalind is the one who makes sure we eat and have clean clothes. She is on top of things—detailed, organized, and meticulous. These are big words for an eight-year-old, but ones she uses so often to describe herself that they have become my spelling words to memorize. Having a strong vocabulary is a must if I want to be a great journalist.

Every day, Rosalind picks me up from school and we go for long walks. We walk through the park and wander about the trees and plants. At night, we spend hours looking at the stars with the help of her super-duper telescope, making up wonderful tales about the planets and our future travels to them.

Now you say how on earth did I have the willpower not to share my secret mission? Well, everyone knows that Clark Kent would never tell, and neither would Stella Dallas.

When I ask Rosalind about Momma, she says that the world is a wonderful and mysterious place and that the universe has a plan and there is no way to predict it. We'll just have to see where it takes us. She says that the one thing I can count on is the love of my family. She always talks about how fortunate we are to have each other, and how our special strengths shine through in all of our activities. She says it is Momma's love and support that has given us the courage to develop these strengths and how she is the best mom a girl could want, or a boy, for that matter. Rosalind is so sure about stuff. I always feel safe around her.

Little did she know that the pain of losing Momma would change everything and rock the ground we stood on and scatter the stars above.

Paul, at fifteen, is a typical teenage boy. He is a good student and athlete. He is either on the phone or busy running around with the newest girlfriend of the week. He is the least involved in what is going on around the house. His iPod is always plugged into his head. He isn't really mean to me; he just doesn't pay much attention. He calls me squirt and gives me money to do his chores. That was until Momma got sick. From the time she started her treatments, he almost disappeared into busyness, never home, or in his room with the door closed. Remember I told you that William is now at Nana and Poppa's, so Paul has his own space. I try going into his room and hanging out, but he just says that I am distracting him from his studies. Right! With the iPod, computer, and texting, I doubt that he could even notice. He never seems to have time to answer my questions, always saying, "Later squirt, I promise."

Later never came…Momma died three years later…Paul never answered even one of my questions.

Age Nine.

During the "year of treatments" (as we call it) life has been, and continues to be, oh-so-different around our house. Momma is always home. Now, I don't know how familiar you are with cancer treatments, but they are weird. They put what they call a port in your chest—"yuck." The medicine then goes in through a needle and into the port. I am not sure how I can stand to know all of these details, but as a journalist, I must prepare myself to hear all kinds of strange things and to be able to report them accurately. So for my first task, I must listen and write with precision (another big word I am proud of).

As you can well imagine, the house is busy as a bee-hive—friends, Nana and Poppa, aunts, and uncles in and out all of the time, everyone fussing and buzzing around Momma, getting her things and keeping her company.

Sometimes I just want to scream, "Everyone go home!" Mostly I just want our family back like it was before... before the cancer.

With everyone so busy, no one is talking about what is happening to our family. Lucky for them, I'm the dedicated journalist.

On the days that Momma gets her medicine through the port, she is at the doctor's office for hours. She comes home and goes straight to bed. Well, I know how tired you get from going to the doctor, so this I understand. When I ask Momma how she is feeling, she tells me that she is fine but tired. She has become better at telling me lies, but I don't challenge her. I have this sense that she needs to do things her own way. I just keep praying and using my superpowers, knowing that as a family, I have us covered. I try very hard to be quiet on these days. I stay in my room and do my homework. I am now in fourth grade, and there is plenty of homework. At other times, I read or bother one of my sisters or brothers to keep me company. Elizabeth has gotten into the habit of reading with me before bed, and I love this. She also looks like something is wrong, but she just smiles and says everything is fine.

On the days Momma doesn't have to go to the doctors (which are few) and between periods of resting, she plays cards with me. She is not happy in the kitchen, saying that the smell of food makes her nauseous (one of the side effects of the treatment). So the big kids are cooking, and most nights, I get to decide what we are eating for dinner.

Dinner is truly the best time of the day. Yes, I love school and all, but spending time in the kitchen and helping with dinner is what I like best. I have a chance to share my day with whoever is in charge of cooking. I can gossip and tell my tales and complaints. I can just go on and on, and nobody seems to care...not like before.

Before Momma got sick, my sisters and brothers would take turns complaining about my constant need to talk about everything. But now, it is as if they like the noise, or maybe they are so preoccupied with what is happening that they just don't notice.

Because William goes to every medical appointment with Momma, he is not around much. After doctor days, he is making up work time in the lab. On no-doctor days, he is also in the lab. Either way, I only see him on Sundays, and I miss him. Sometimes he forgets to call me cutie pie. He looks so sad. I think this is the hardest on him.

One night as Elizabeth and I were getting ready to read, I asked if we could update our interview. I wanted to know, now that almost a year had passed, what she was thinking. Elizabeth said that she thought the year was going quite well and that as a team we were doing a good job taking care of business. She said that it is difficult to see Momma sick, but she has great hopes that the treatments will work and Momma will get better and be her old self again. I told her, "Me too." As always, we hugged, kissed, read, and, finally, I went to sleep.

When I look back, now at age thirteen, I am a bit surprised that no one thought this little girl might be afraid or sad. No one ever asked how I was feeling. I guess they bought my lies, the same way they bought Momma's. But I knew the truth for both of us.

Age Eleven

Winter

Unfortunately, the "year of treatments" continues on and on. Once they started, they never stopped. There were times that I'd forget to write or interview. Everyone was busy, and the days just rolled on. When I'd ask what was new, the famous answer was "same old, same old." So I stopped asking and stopped writing, that is until now.

The weather is horrible. It has been a cold, dark winter. I'm miserable, and so is everyone else in the house. Momma spends her days and nights in bed; she never leaves her room. We take turns visiting her, sitting on her bed, and reporting about our days. She puts on a small smile and says, "Oh." I sit outside her door and listen when my sisters and brothers go in, just to see if Momma is more interested in their stuff, being they are older and doing all kinds of fun things. I only have school stuff to talk about, and after four older kids, I'm sure mine is boring. But the only sound I hear is of my sisters and brothers talking and Momma saying, "Oh." At other times, I crawl into bed with Momma and we watch television. Because it is difficult for her to put her arm around me, we just hold hands. Now, Momma is very thin. She doesn't really look the same anymore, but when she smiles, she is still Momma. And when she asks about homework and grades, she is definitely still Momma.

When Momma is not too tired, I read to her. I love to read, and this is a good chance for me to entertain Momma and practice my reading aloud skills. I know that as a journalist there will be times that I have to talk and not just write. This practice will serve me well.

It doesn't matter how tired she is, Momma always tells me that she loves me and that she is proud of me. She makes me promise to listen to my sisters and brothers and to always work hard and do my best. Now please don't misunderstand me—I love time with Momma, but I can't help thinking, *yeah, yeah, yeah*, as I roll my eyes. Compared to my friends, I am an angel. My momma is clueless.

Late at night, I can hear Elizabeth, Rosalind, and William talking in whispers, discussing Momma's treatments, her illness, and the household problems. Actually, there are few problems, except with Paul. He refuses to be home or participate in much of anything except Sunday dinner. Momma can no longer come to the table, so we take dinner into her room. We sit on the floor playing soft music, talking, and laughing. Momma just listens as the rest of us carry on. Paul just eats and runs.

My sisters do a great job of keeping Momma's room bright and cheerful with beautiful flower arrangements that are free from smells. Momma says that the strong sweet smells give her a headache and make her sick to her stomach. I hope that never happens to me. I love to smell flowers. Momma's bed has the most magnificent old velvet shawl draped over it. The shawl belonged to Momma's grandmother and is by far Momma's most favorite possession.

Before Momma was sick, she would tell us stories about her grandmother, stories about the old country, Russia, before the war. There were just a few things that her grandmother was able to bring on her journey from Russia. Momma has this shawl and a pair of candlestick holders that sit on her dresser. My sisters used to argue over who was going to inherit the shawl and candlesticks. I could never understand what the fuss was about. But now, I think I am beginning to understand. The arguments have stopped, and there is no mention of the shawl or candlesticks.

I am the only one who knows, that late at night Paul sneaks into Momma's room. He never stays long, but I know that Momma loves it. Later on, after these visits, I can hear him quietly sobbing in his bedroom. You see, I'm not sleeping much. As the family reporter, I feel an obligation to listen, watch, and record all activities, so sleep is not in the formula. I only go to sleep when I am falling over. Everyone thinks I'm sleeping—after all, they tuck me in—but I don't stay there, and they don't notice. By now, everyone looks tired and sad. But, day by day, we keep our routines going as if somehow we have become robots.

Age Eleven

Spring

I'd been waiting and waiting for spring, hoping that the sun would bring some smiles and happiness to my family. But, I was wrong. Then, as if out of the blue, William called for a family meeting. Even Paul showed up, so I knew this was very serious and not good. William went on to tell us that the doctor had done everything he could do for Momma, but she was not getting better. Now, everyone was crying. I held my head in my hands; Elizabeth held me on one side, Rosalind on the other, while William wrapped his arms around Paul. There was silence; no one said a word until I asked, "Is Momma dying?" William quietly whispered, "Yes."

I thought my heart would burst out of my chest. I felt a terrible warm stabbing feeling, like a knife had just been pushed into my body. All we could do was cry. William continued, through his tears, to be our leader. He explained that the doctor had a long talk with him and Momma, and that Momma asked him to tell the family. He said that he wanted to tell all of us first, and then he would tell Nana and Poppa, and everyone else. He said that Momma wanted us to be strong, to stick together ("like glue," I added), and to make her proud. He told Paul and me that he, Elizabeth, and Rosalind would include us in all decisions and plans. I cried out, "Decisions and plans, what are you talking about?" My mind started spinning. William promised me that nothing would change after Momma died. We would still live together, I would still go to the same school, and we would still be sisters and brothers taking care of one another.

After a short time, everyone just sort of walked away. We all needed some time and space.

I spent the rest of the day and night in my room confused, afraid, and unsure of what was going to happen. I went to sleep hoping that things would be different in the morning. Maybe all of this would turn out to be a big mistake or a terrible nightmare. But it isn't...and today is not any better. I keep asking myself—how could my plan have gone so wrong—what happened to all of my prayers and superpower—what is wrong with me that I failed my mission that I failed my momma—that I failed the people who love me more than anything in the world my family?

I can't tell anyone about my failure. I know that if one of my sisters or brothers learn about my failure, they will tell one another, and they will hate me. What would I do if they didn't love me anymore?

So I kept my secret. Momma died shortly after that meeting.

I can hardly describe the events surrounding Momma's death and funeral. Momma and William had handled all of what they called "the arrangements." Elizabeth and Rosalind agreed to whatever Momma wanted. Paul and I were just along for the ride. If you have never been to a funeral, you are lucky. I still can't talk about it. It still seems like a nightmare, not because it was so scary, but because saying good-bye to Momma was so hard. My sisters and brothers kept telling me how important it was to honor Momma by the rituals of the funeral and service. They talked nonstop about us as a family— sticking together in good times and bad, and being able to tackle any rough times or anything life throws our way. They told me that my job was to trust them and that this is what families do for each other. I guess that my sisters and brothers know stuff that I don't.

The most important time, for me, was during the honorary service. The service was held in the backyard of our best friend's house. This was Momma's wish. We were to meet outside, during the day, having lots of food and drinks, and especially desserts. She wanted flowers everywhere and, of course, music. Now this may sound like it could be a party, so I am not really sure about anything. During this service/party, everyone had a chance to say something about Momma. I think they were all shocked when I got up on a chair, raised my glass of soda, and shouted, "To the best momma ever—don't forget me...I love you...Stella." I think I was a bit shocked too. But then, everybody applauded, and more sweet things were said about Momma.

Since the service/party, things have been uneventful. We have stepped right back into our daily activities; Paul and I returning to our classes, and the others returning to work. Things at home don't seem all that different, except for the empty feeling in the house. When I come home from school all excited to tell Momma about something stupid, like a grade, I remember, she isn't here. At first, there were lots of people visiting and dropping by. Then slowly, they stopped. Nana and Poppa come by regularly, but they are so sad, it is almost worse when they are here. Gradually, I am not sure when or how, but, I've stopped talking. I really don't have much to say. I no longer help with dinner and don't care what we have. I spend most of my time in my room reading. Since no one is complaining, I guess they think this is a phase that will pass.

Well, it didn't...at least it didn't until now.

Age Thirteen

Part One

It is as if I woke up—I'm thirteen and feel it's time to rejoin the family. I think Momma has probably forgiven me for not being strong enough to save her…at least I hope she has.

Elizabeth and Rosalind have been telling me for two years now that Momma would want me to do things, that Momma would want me to enjoy my life…but how, I ask?

Then finally the most amazing thing happened. One day, as Rosalind and I were out walking (we still do this together), she started crying. As we hugged, she confessed that despite hours of praying, she couldn't get Momma better. She said that she was terribly sad and missed Momma more than anything in the world—and felt heartbroken for Paul and me having to lose Momma while we were so young. She went on to say how she prayed and prayed, but nothing came of it. It was then that I told her my horrible disgrace. After much crying and hugging, she explained that we were not responsible for Momma's death and that accepting she is gone is difficult for all of us. She said a lot of other things. She talked for a long time, but I can't remember it all. What I know is that she said it was not my fault and she didn't blame me. She convinced me to talk to Elizabeth and William to see how they felt.

The next night, everyone gathered except Paul who was out (as usual). Elizabeth, Rosalind, and William cried and told me similar stories of praying and similar stories of disappointment. And of course, they didn't blame me for anything. I guess, being grown-up and everything, they know stuff I don't. They begged me to believe them. I told them that believing them was a problem because of the secrets during Momma's illness. They understood. Nobody laughed at me. They are truly great siblings. They promised that in the future, from this point forward, that no matter what the issue or problem, they would include me in the discussions. They realized that by leaving me out and attempting to protect me, they were actually making things harder for me.

With my new freedom, it is time for me to do all of the things that Momma wanted (that is according to my sisters and brothers). So it is off to high school for me and one last interview for my family.

After much thought, I decided to start my interviews in a highly professional manner. I wrote questions, considered how I should ask them, thought about each family member, and tried to anticipate how different their responses would be. I also decided to record the interviews like they do on television. This way I can practice and review my journalist skills. Presentation is very important, you know. Everyone always comments on the interviewer, as well as the person being interviewed.

All dressed up in a nice skirt, T-shirt, and borrowed scarf from Elizabeth, I set the stage. I put two chairs in my room, facing each other, and set up the video recorder. On a small table next to the chairs sat a box of tissues and two glasses of water (standard interview necessities). My notes were neatly placed on my lap. My serious face and smile, having rehearsed in front of the mirror, were ready to go.

As before, I decided to start with my oldest sister, Elizabeth.

Stella: What is your best memory of Momma?

Elizabeth: Oh, Stella, there are so many. One of my favorites was when I graduated from college. It felt like a miracle the way Momma managed to set aside an entire day for us to spend together. Usually, between work, chores, and the family, there was rarely a free moment. I was thrilled and delighted to have Momma all to myself. We started the day with breakfast at a great little downtown restaurant. Momma made a point of finding all unique places for us that day, our special time.

OK, here come the tears. Good thing for the tissues, or we'd have to stop.

> After breakfast, we went shopping for work clothes and shoes. I knew that there really wasn't extra money for this day and appreciated that Momma must have been saving for this occasion for some time. She insisted on buying me this beautiful briefcase, so that I'd be ready to start my professional life feeling and looking confident. This was truly one of the dearest things Momma ever did for me. Stella, I will use this briefcase until it falls apart and then some. After shopping, we did what we always did best—have dessert.

Stella: How is it being the oldest in the family?

Elizabeth: For the most part, it has been a pleasure. With Momma gone, I feel a deep sense of pride that I was able to help her raise you kids, and ultimately, feel very connected to all of you. It was important for me to earn Momma's respect and trust. She was always setting a high standard for me to live up to. As a younger child, there were times that I just wanted to be left alone, not bothered with anything or anybody. It was those times that I was resentful. But those times were short-lived because Momma would be so happy, cracking jokes, playing music, popping popcorn, or pulling us into a game of Monopoly. She had a wonderful way of making me laugh and encouraging me to have fun, without sacrificing my focus on school and the family. She always told me that her kids were the joy of her life.

Stella: What are your worst memories?

Elizabeth: When Momma was dying. (*Here go the tears again.*) Stella, there were times that I was not sure how to go on. It was heartbreaking to see her so sick and, for the first time in my life, to see her so sad.

Stella: Momma sad! What a shock. I didn't know.

I better watch myself... almost lost my journalist's cool.

Elizabeth: Of course she was sad. She didn't want to leave us. She worried about all of us, but she worried mostly about you and Paul. Being the youngest two, she was worried and sad that she would not be here to help you grow up. Little did she know that even though I was an adult, I still needed her too! We all needed her. Maybe you never stop needing your mom. Stella, I was going to wait until you turned sixteen, but I guess this is as good a time as ever, Momma left you a letter. Would you like to have it?

Oh no, I am the interviewer; this is turning out all wrong.

Stella: A letter?

Elizabeth: Yes, Momma wrote one to each of us.

Stella: Have you read your letter?

Elizabeth: I read it every night. It helps me feel like Momma is with me.

Stella: Does it freak you out and make you cry?

Elizabeth: I do cry some, but it is also comforting. There is also something else, Stella. Momma left a special piece of jewelry for you, for when you are older. She wanted to make sure that she could encourage and empower you through your most difficult times. I can show you the jewelry, but it is for when you turn eighteen.

Stella: That's OK. I think we should stop now.

Boy, do I have a lot to think about. I need to clear my mind, change my clothes, and get some fresh air. What am I going to do? Momma sad, letters, jewelry—I guess I didn't anticipate this information. Maybe this is what happens as a journalist, surprise stuff. If I am ever going to do this job, I have to get better at this interview thing. Now, the jewelry part sounds fun, but waiting until eighteen doesn't. Nothing feels or seems right anymore.

Just when I think things are moving along—bam—I am back to where I started, confused, lost, and dazed. There are moments in school when the time just seems to pass, like a daydream. One minute I am listening to the teacher, and the next minute I am gone. When I return, I've missed a beat, and I don't even know what it is. It has been a real challenge in school, this daydreaming thing. It never happened when Momma was alive. But now, I never know when it will take over. I can be in school, spending time with friends or playing a game and then, poof, I am gone. As you can well imagine, when this happens, people get annoyed. Friends call me airhead. My teacher is forever saying, "Stella, pay attention." My family is starting to think I'm ditsy. Nana says it is just a normal part of being a teenager. I just feel empty. On the outside, I can laugh, joke, play, eat, sleep, and look OK. But on the inside, I am not sure I exist anymore. The joy I used to feel, so light and carefree, is now heavy, empty, and dark.

When I think about Momma, it used to be like a knife was cutting me open, sharp and hard. Now, it feels like a continual dull ache, always there and never going away. What nobody knows is that I think about her all of the time. I expect her to be home when I get there, and I am shocked that she isn't.

When my friends talk about their mom, or I see them, I cringe and feel like I am going to throw up. At night, when I close my eyes, I see Momma and I dream about the things we used to do. There are people on talk shows that say their parents visit them in their dreams—pretty scary—so for a while, I didn't want to go to sleep. But Momma has not made that visit to me. Oh, a question I forgot to ask Elizabeth. I bet if Momma visited anyone it would be Rosalind. I will put that on her list of questions.

Now that I think about it, if Momma wrote letters, she must have known she was dying. How creepy is that! I wonder what it felt like dying. I wonder where Momma went. Is she somewhere watching? Will I ever see her again? I still don't understand why my prayers didn't work to save her. I guess I am just plain sad…sad like Momma.

Age Thirteen

Part Two

It has taken me a bit of time to recover from Elizabeth's interview. I thought I knew how much I missed Momma, but talking to Elizabeth really hit hard.

During this time, I have tried to be the best journalist ever by reading about death, dying, and grief. There really isn't much for kids to read and some of it is soo...well... babyish. But there is one book, about kids' grief after a parent dies that is pretty good. This book is special; it was written by kids with the help of an adult, and the adult lost her mom when she was—you got it—eleven, just like me.

Reading this book took my breath away—it was like looking into a mirror.

What I didn't believe, didn't want to believe, was how hard and long this grieving would be. In my heart, I knew that things would never be the same. But, wow, I didn't really understand, and neither did anyone else in my family.

The most shocking part of the book is something called the timeline. I must have read this section a hundred times. I am still not sure I get it. I haven't shared this book with anyone yet.

As a resourceful journalist, I found this book on Amazon, went to the bookstore, and bought it with my own money. I really need someone to do this with me and decided that William is my best bet. Elizabeth is too emotional, Rosalind too mystical, and Paul…well, Paul is simply not there (even though he is nicer to me since Momma died). At times, he comes into my room just to say hi. He asks if he can help with my homework, and on special occasions, he takes me for pizza or ice cream. Of course, we never talk about anything; he is just so quiet. But you know me; I can go on and on. Paul just laughs and calls me squirt.

Since William is the next in line to be interviewed, the timing is perfect. William, as busy as he is, always makes time for anyone who needs it. He agreed to Saturday afternoon, outside in the backyard, with iced tea and cookies, and then I can complete my task. Work first and then pleasure, he always says. Well, my problem with this grief stuff overshadowed my desire for fun, but it also isn't the task, so it comes second.

Stella: William, since I was so young when Momma got sick, I'm not sure I know much about it. Can you tell me about Momma, the cancer, and the treatments?

William: All right. Cancer is a disease about the body malfunctioning. For some reason, which we don't fully understand, the cells in the body go wild. They reproduce and reproduce and turn into bad cells. These bad cells form into large groups called tumors and eventually gang up on all of the good cells. Any questions?

Stella: Yes, about the doctors. How do they help you get better?

William: There are many treatments that the doctors use, and some people do get better. Do you remember watching the bike races with Lance Armstrong? He is a good example of someone getting better after cancer treatments.

But for others, like Momma, the bad cells are so strong that the medicine and treatments can't stop them from growing and taking over. I'm not sure how much you remember, but Momma had every treatment possible. First she had surgery, and then chemotherapy medicines, and then something called radiation, where a machine beams radiation into the tumor cells.

Stella: That sounds like something from a science fiction movie.

William: The machines look like that too.

Oh no, there goes my journalistic professionalism. As William talked, flashes of those treatment times flew before my eyes. I couldn't help but see Momma sick and sad. I started crying like a baby. I couldn't help myself. William was so nice—he held me, and kissed me, and told me he felt the same way, as tears rolled down his face. William went on to tell me that he spent a lot of time with Momma at doctor appointments and in the car traveling back and forth. He said that this was the hardest time in his life, and some of the best. That during this special time with Momma, they talked nonstop.

William: We always talked about the cancer and treatments and how kind the doctors were. Momma always wanted to know if I agreed with the treatments. And of course, since I was keeping up with the new medical advances and research, I could comfort her with a yes. The doctors and I had long discussions about Momma's treatments, ensuring that we were doing everything possible to get her better.

Stella: Was it very scary at the doctor's office?

William: No, but sitting here now, with you, I bet you were scared.

Stella: I was.

William: Stella, I am so sorry that we didn't take you with us sometimes. I guess nobody realized how frightened you were and how going to the doctor with us could have helped relieve some of your fears.

Stella: I think you're right. It would have helped me. William, how do you get cancer?

William: OK, well let's see…no one knows exactly. The body simply malfunctions.

Stella: Can you catch cancer like a cold?

William: No, you can't.

Stella: So how do you know if you have it?

William: Not to worry cutie pie, it is my job to make sure you stay healthy and get regular checkups.

Stella: What about Elizabeth, Rosalind, Paul, and you?

William: We are also keeping up with our yearly healthy checkups. What I am sure about is that between the three of us older kids, and Paul, there will always be someone to take care of you, love you, and help you grow up. Medical science is actively working at developing new medicines and treatments in hopes that someday everyone with cancer will get better.

Stella, I'd like to tell you more about my conversations with Momma, would you like to hear them?

Stella: Yes, but I know I will cry — it makes me so sad.

William: Me too, but it also makes me feel warm and loved to talk about her, so let's try to go on for a bit. Usually during her treatments or in the car ride home, Momma and I would talk up a storm remembering stories from my childhood. The funny things I did as a little boy, my science experiments, and how early each of us developed strong interests. Momma always talked about how proud she was of all her kids. How different life was with our dad, and even though she was left alone with us, she never felt alone.

She talked about her parents and what a comfort they were, and how they offered us this wonderful, great support system. But even more than that, she said it was all of us and our love and devotion to one another that made everything OK. We talked about how this came about to be. How was it that, as a family, we shared so much love and dedication? Momma described the important role that our large extended family, of grandparents, aunts, uncles, and cousins, played by offering us a safety net of security and stability. Being surrounded by family ensured that there was always somebody nearby to help, visit, or play with. She also felt that we were lucky to be smart. Our love for education, having numerous interests, and being interested in the world was what she admired and enjoyed about us the most. The one good thing about Dad, she always said, was how smart he was, and how his best accomplishment was passing on the smart genes. She liked to joke about how she made up for the rest— the heart, love, caring, and creative genes. Of course, Momma was exceptionally smart too. I think she felt a sense of obligation to give Dad credit for something. Momma always talked about you and Paul. She couldn't help but worry about the two of you growing up without her, even though she trusted Elizabeth, Rosalind, and me to be great surrogate parents.

Stella: What is a surrogate?

William: A surrogate is a substitute. Even though Momma knew we would love you and take good care of you, she was very sad that she could not be here to see you and Paul grow up.

Stella: William, I need a favor. In my efforts to be the best journalist ever, I started reading about death and dying, and kids whose parent died. There are some things I don't understand and was hoping you could read this one book and explain some things. It is a great book. When you read it, pay special attention to something they call the timeline. It is really confusing.

William: I'd be honored to help you, Stella. Give me a couple of hours to read the book.

Stella: One last question, William. Did Momma leave letters for all of us, and have you read yours?

William: Yes, she did…and yes, I have.

Silence! Now what am I supposed to say?

William: These letters are special and very dear, Stella. When I need to be close to Momma, I read some of it or all of it. The letters afford each of us a private time with Momma.

Stella: I hadn't thought about you, Elizabeth, and Rosalind needing to be close to Momma. When I need to be close to her, I hold her picture close to my heart.

As tears poured out of my eyes, I confided in William.

Stella: No one knows this, William, but at night, most nights, I sleep with Momma's picture in my bed, and I almost always wear one of her T-shirts to sleep.

William: Just like Momma would say, this is a good time for an ice cream break. What do you think?

Stella: I think I'm hungry. How about pizza and then ice cream?

William: Sounds perfect.

I guess William is not going to share his letter with me. I am not sure when I'll be ready to read mine. For right now, these interviews are enough. Maybe that's what Momma meant when she'd say, "Let sleeping dogs lie."

Later that evening, William approached me about the book on grief. His eyes were all red, and I could tell he had been crying. He told me that the book was very painful to read. The kids' stories of loss, of sadness, of missing their parents were overwhelming, and he didn't know how I managed to read them.

The timeline, he explained, demonstrates how grief goes up and down, and round and round, like a roller coaster. For about the first six months everyone is in shock, and then this unbelievable sadness sets in. However, as time rolls on, the never-ending sadness moves like the ocean—from strong waves to quiet ripples, to strong waves and quiet ripples, and so on and so on. This means that there are times of deep sadness and days that are filled with pleasure, fun, and minimal sadness, or almost no sadness. It seems that it is the length of time without your parent that hits the kids the hardest. William ended his explanation by saying that the grief timeline was no different for adult children.

I replied, "I was afraid of that."

There wasn't much else to say...There really was so much more to say. We just couldn't find the words, not yet.

A week has passed, and I feel ready to start again. I've spent this week looking over my interviews with Elizabeth and William to ensure that I have fresh new questions for Rosalind. This is called covering your bases. By the way, I am surprised at how much better I'm sleeping and feeling since I started these interviews. Yesterday I was with friends, smiling and laughing, almost like old times. My best friend gave me a hug, and told me how glad she was to be having fun with me again. When I went home, I thought about this. After all, I'm Momma's daughter, thinking and caring about life and what happens are important personal traits. I am realizing that even though I like to talk a lot, I do a pretty good job of listening.

My goal of getting these interviews done before high school begins is approaching quickly. The problem, you see, is that I felt so good after William's interview, I almost forgot I had more to do…well, not really forgot.

This was the first time since Momma's death that I felt a bit like me, the old me. It was just flakes, bits, and pieces, but there were days where I laughed and smiled easily, like before. At night, I could kiss Momma's picture and feel at peace. But that didn't last long. Then, all of a sudden, I could feel the sadness and anger creeping over me like a shadow. It seems to me that I am now two people, the old me and the new me, sprinkled with grains of sadness that rub and irritate. At other times, the sand covers all of my life, quiet and still. Memories of Momma are better now. I remember her with a smile on her face, enjoying our family. I remember our fun times, and seldom think about her when she was sick.

One day Nana and Poppa were over for dinner, and everyone was telling funny stories about Momma. Laughing out loud, I shouted, "I love these stories and almost never think about Momma sick." Nana told me that time is sometimes our friend, that time is like a strainer—shaking out the bad memories, leaving only the good ones.

Unfortunately, duty calls. It's time to get back to my interviews.

For Rosalind's interview, I decided to move the stage outside, at night, under the stars, definitely Rosalind's favorite place. Good interviewers know that if you want to get interesting information, you have to make the person you are interviewing as comfortable as possible. Elizabeth is always talking to me about what qualities make for a great interview. She always says, "If people are relaxed, they are going to give you more information, and the conversation will flow easier" (*whatever that means*).

Keeping true to my professional status, the water and tissues were set up on a small table between our chairs. I also put blankets on the chairs just in case. You know, it can get chilly outside at night, and I wanted to make sure nothing disturbed this important interview. I needed Rosalind in the best mood possible for my most intimate questions.

Stella: Rosalind, this is the best. The stars are bright, and it is so quiet.

Rosalind: I love this time of the day best.

Stella: Rosalind, tell me about Momma.

Rosalind: Stella, I think in some ways, I had a special relationship with Momma. We were alike in many ways. I don't know if anyone has told you, but as a teenager, Momma was called a hippie. Wait here I have some pictures.

As Rosalind ran to her room, I was amazed at how many things I didn't know.

Rosalind: Oh, Stella, look at this picture of Momma—she must be about sixteen, so beautiful with long, dark, curly hair, and so happy. Momma used to tell me stories about her beliefs in the wonderment of life…how she and her friends would spend hours stargazing, contemplating the planets, discussing the possibility of life existing on other planets, discussing their ideas about religion and God, discussing the meaning of life and how we are all connected to one another in mysterious ways.

Momma loved to read, and fortunately for me, we shared this passion. We'd read all different kinds of books and then have long conversations and debates about the hidden messages and meanings. I loved Alice Hoffman with her stories of mystical magic, and scientists like Einstein and Galileo. Momma loved Anne Rice with her odd sensational stories, and savored her books by great and influential thinkers like Freud, Carl Jung, Viktor Frankl, Elie Wiesel, Martin Buber, Eleanor Roosevelt and Golda Meir—just to name a few.

When we discussed these books, Momma would ask me to picture myself as curious as these masters. She'd describe each and every one of these masters as having had different and unique ways of viewing the world, having developed original ideas, questioning and challenging existing thoughts, and never being satisfied with the status quo as a solution.

Stella: Status quo?

Rosalind; Status quo is the typical, accepted, usual, and ordinary or standard way to do things or think about things. Stella, if you learn nothing else about our mother, you can be assured she was anything but ordinary. Whenever I told Momma something, she always wanted to know more. How did I come to that decision, was I pleased with it, did it turn out the way I planned, and if not, why? Momma made me stretch my thinking, and, ultimately, I fell in love with the things she read.

My best time with Momma was when I had her all to myself—cooking, walking, or sitting up late at night, outside, just like now…just like you and me.

Stella: I never knew that.

Rosalind: You were probably asleep by that time. If you'd like, I can show you Momma's favorite books, and when you feel ready, we can continue this tradition. We can have our own book club.

Stella: Rosalind, I saved this question just for you. Did Momma ever talk about dying? I know I was very young, but when I think back, I can't imagine going through such a big thing without talking about it.

Rosalind: Momma and I had lots of late night talks about dying. Momma was very spiritual. She felt that we are all connected in ways that transcend this physical life. She believed that everyone's spirit, soul, and being lives on for eternity, even after the body is no longer usable.

Stella: Was Momma scared?

Rosalind: No. She would tell me that she just didn't feel ready to leave us. She felt as if her job of raising her kids was not complete. If she could have only lived till you and Paul were all grown, she'd feel more peaceful.

Now this sounds familiar. I guess Momma really meant this. I've heard this twice before.

Rosalind: Momma was forever talking about how proud she was of all of us. She described feeling confident that Elizabeth, William, and I had learned and accepted her wishes, desires, and lifestyle—satisfied that we three would be great parents to you and Paul—and comforted in knowing that we would pass on all of her important life lessons and expectations. Stella, I can't tell you enough how much Momma loved you…loved all of us. She was proud of us, and believed that we would grow up to be productive, loving, great people who would take care of each other and contribute to the community and the world. Together, Momma and I picked special stars to wish on. We agreed that when I was lonely, I could reach out to our stars and she'd smile down at me. *(With this, Rosalind started to cry.)* I know you are young, Stella, but I wondered how I was going to live my life without Momma. She was my idol and the center of my universe.

Silence

Now what? I find myself, Stella, thirteen-years-old, holding my older sister Rosalind, patting her back as she wept in my arms. Rosalind doesn't realize that she is my rock. I feel more loved and closer to Momma when I am with her. It was Rosalind who held me during the funeral, and it is in Rosalind's bed that I now go to in the middle of the night when I have bad dreams. It is Rosalind who hums songs and sings to me and lights candles in the bathroom and prepares special lavender baths to help me feel calm and relaxed. It is Rosalind who brews special tea to help me concentrate. It is Rosalind who puts fresh flowers in my bedroom in Momma's favorite vase, just as Momma always did. I guess she is the one who will keep our favorite traditions.

Rosalind always tells me that even though Momma is not here physically, she is here in spirit and deed. So we follow her traditions, from dinners, to table linens, to outings, to shopping and cleaning. Momma's way has now become our way.

The one big exception is the music that vibrates within the house. With all of our different tastes, you never know what to expect when you walk in the door. If you know whose turn it is to choose that day's music, you can pretty well guess what you are in for. Not surprisingly, I get teased the most about my music. What my siblings don't know is that finding new musical groups has become a bit of a hobby. With so many older, smarter, and wiser siblings, this is one arena I can be the most knowledge-able about. In our home, music is a must. There is always music playing, "Always was and always will be" (those are Rosalind's words).

The other noticeable family change is in the variety of food found in the refrigerator and cupboard. Rosalind and I have become quite adventurous in the kitchen, collecting recipes and bringing them to life. For the most part, we are decent chefs.

Of course, the biggest change revolves around the holidays. Nobody can bear the holidays…these are the saddest times for us. We couldn't tolerate celebrating the holidays in the same ways; even Rosalind couldn't pretend to find comfort in Momma having a spirit. During the holidays, Momma's absence is unavoidable. These are the times that I am the angriest. Even now, two years later, I feel no better about the holidays. I can't imagine that I ever will.

The newest holiday ritual is our donation basket. I don't remember whose idea it was, but we somehow decided that since we couldn't give Momma gifts, we could still buy gifts and give them to charities in Momma's name. It is called "In Honor Of." Each of us gets to pick what charity we want to give to, and as a family, we vote on one for each holiday. Before delivering the gifts, we go to the cemetery and present the basket to Momma and leave her flowers. The charities with kids are always my favorite, especially since we can buy toys. But of course, people who are in need of food and clothing must come first.

At holidays, we realize that with all of our pain and sadness, we are fortunate to have one another. I have the best sisters and brothers a girl could want.

Stella: Rosalind, I need to ask you about your dreams. Does Momma ever visit you in them? I've been waiting, but she hasn't come to me yet.

Rosalind: No, Stella, the only dreams I have of Momma are my memories or wishes. This place here, in my heart, and up in the stars is where Momma is for me. Stella, I am sorry that I never thought about making sure you had a special place too. I think we were all so busy taking care of things when Momma was dying that some things fell through the cracks. How about if I make sure you come out at night with me and find her star. In fact, let's find it right now. Search the sky and let your eyes wander about. Eventually, one of the stars will catch your attention and interest. The star that feels special, that warms your heart, will become your special star. You can reach out and have Momma close to you anytime you'd like.

All I could do was smile and enjoy the night sky's entertainment. Finally, the words that were most important and most scary found their way out.

Stella: Rosalind, did Momma write you a letter?

Rosalind; She left a letter for each of us, Stella. Would you like to see yours?

I don't know what came over me...I started to cry. Rosalind held me and rubbed my back. I looked up through my tears at my special star and imagined Momma watching and smiling and crying too. She must be lonely and miss us also...I hope she is OK...I hope she knows I love her... I hope she knows that I am no longer angry that she died and left me. Though, I am still sad...and...still...everyday wish she was here.

Wow, this last interview took me by surprise. I thought that my older siblings had things under control. I had no idea how they were feeling.

Maybe Paul is feeling the same way. I decided to do his interview differently. Late one night, after everyone settled into their evening routine, I tiptoed into Paul's room and asked if we could talk. Of course, I had to ask him to shut off his iPod and actually look at me, instead of the computer screen. When he turned around, I was curled up on his bed covered in Momma's favorite throw blanket. I think Paul recognized how much I needed him at this moment in time. He moved his chair right up to the bed and said, "Fire away squirt." I told him that I had interviewed Elizabeth, William, and Rosalind about Momma and wanted to talk to him about some stuff.

Let's not forget, Paul is now twenty. He is still very quiet and spends most of his free time with his friends or in his room. Over the years, he has become more involved in the family. When everyone else is busy working, he helps with household chores, food shopping, preparing meals, and of course driving me around town.

I started talking rather than asking questions. That's how it was with us. I told him all about the other interviews. The questions I asked and the answers I received.

Finally, after what felt like hours, I asked him my first question.

Stella: Paul, do you think about Momma?

Paul: All of the time, Stella.

Silence

OK, this is going to be like pulling teeth. I had hoped that after all that sharing he would be ready to talk...Right!

Stella: Paul, you are so quiet—it would help me to know how you feel and what you are thinking. Do you talk to anybody?

Silence

If it is the last thing I do, I am determined to remain quiet and wait. After some time, Paul started.

Paul: Stella, through the years, I have confided in several friends, but only the friends who cared enough or were brave enough and genuine enough to ask if I was OK. But I do have a secret I will share with you. I have never told anyone— before Momma died, I would go into her room at night.

Stella: I know, Paul. I didn't sleep much during that time and would hear you go down the hall to her room. I always wondered what you were talking about.

Paul: Stella, as you know, Momma was very wise. She knew me better than anyone ever will. She made me promise that after she died I would keep a journal. That I would write my days' events, thoughts, and feelings, as if I was writing to her, as if I was talking to her, just like those late night talks. And so, I have been writing. I write letters to Momma. That is who I talk to, Stella.

Stella: Does it make you sad and cry?

Paul: Sometimes. But I promised Momma.

Stella: Are there other things you promised her?

Paul: Yes. I promised her that I would continue in school and do my best, that I would not let my heartache or her death stop me from achieving and fulfilling my life goals, and that I would make her proud and honor her memory by how I lived my life. She also made me promise to stay close to William and the girls, and to watch out for you and be there whenever you needed me. Stella, you probably don't realize that all of us have stayed home since Momma's illness and death. I go to the local university, Rosalind went to the local university for graduate school and is now teaching there, and Elizabeth and William have maintained jobs in town. At some unspoken level, we have all made this commitment to Momma and the family. We have all found a way to make her proud, to become successful people, and to stay together in this house. Stella, I think we did this for you, to help you grow up. But… also…I think we could not bear the idea of being separated from each other cither.

Silence

I had never heard so many words come out of Paul's mouth at one time. In shock and crying, and possibly for the first time in my life, I had nothing to say. But of course, after a short minute, words rolled out of my mouth.

Stella: Paul, I love you.

With that, Paul sat next to me on the bed and held me. He told me that he would always be there for me, even when we were grown up and even if we were not living in the same house. He said that he was proud to be my brother, and that Momma would be proud of me and of my interviews. He then carried me into my bedroom, wrapped in Momma's favorite throw blanket, and tucked me in. I closed my eyes and fell asleep dreaming about Momma.

Momma's Letter

Part One

In the morning after Paul's interview, I realized that I hadn't asked him about his letter from Momma. I knew that I didn't have to. I was sure he had read his, and like the others, I was sure he wasn't going to show it to me. It is probably time for me to read my letter.

That night I asked Elizabeth for my letter. Holding the letter in my hands was so weird. Momma had not only written this, but it may have been one of the last things she touched. I held it as if it could break. I set up a special place outside, under the stars, with a lantern, Momma's favorite throw blanket, and of course a big box of tissues. At the dinner table, I announced that I had a special project to do that evening and needed my privacy. I wanted to make sure nobody disturbed my time with Momma.

I sat outside for what seemed like forever just staring at the envelope. How beautiful it was, covered with pink flowers, and my name, Stella, in Momma's beautiful writing.

To my darling daughter Stella,

Words cannot express how much I love you. After years of not expecting to have any more children, you entered my life, happy, busy, cheerful, and talkative, with so much to say. I think this is what I enjoy most about you. Stella, you have so many amazing qualities. I admire how much you think and care about things, always wanting answers, and always asking questions. I know that your sisters and brothers get annoyed at times, but don't stop! Being inquisitive and curious will get you far in this lifetime.

Stella, an aura of magnetism surrounds you. Since you were a little girl, people have been drawn to you. You are what they call a showstopper. These qualities will also get you far in life.

Your letter is the hardest one for me to write. By now, I am sure you know that I have written to all of your sisters and brothers. You are so young, and there are so many things we didn't get to talk about. I will try to give you as many of these thoughts and wishes as I can in this letter. Your sisters and brothers have so much to offer you; I trust that they will fill in for me.

You are very fortunate to have grown sisters and brothers to share your life with. I can't imagine how I can possibly write, in this small space, everything I need and want you to know, all of life's lessons and all of my thoughts and wishes. Thankfully, Elizabeth, Rosalind, and William have heard enough from me over the years that there isn't too much they can't recite by heart.

I feel a bit lost as to how to begin to guide and parent you through life with only some short words and paragraphs. My heart aches for all of your firsts that I will miss. I will mostly miss seeing you smile when you are happy, and holding you when you are sad. I am so grateful that you have two wonderful women, Elizabeth and Rosalind, to do this for you. They love you dearly.

I had to think long and hard about all of the wishes and dreams I have for you, just especially for you, Stella. Even though you are one of five, you are unique. All during my illness (our illness), you had a way of bringing everyone together, keeping the family busy with daily routines, and keeping the family at home.

Everyone, especially me, benefited from the family spending so much time at home. Since I was housebound for such a long period of time, it was comforting to have all of my kids around. The hustle and bustle of activity helped me a great deal, and kept a smile on my face. I loved hearing the music, the sounds of clanking in the kitchen, and the sound of your voice telling stories and jokes.

You see, Stella, without you, the older kids might have spent more time at school or work, and in general, doing things outside of the house. Because of you, there was a good reason to be home. Because of you, everyone was busy with kid stuff and found lots of reasons to laugh. Thank you my dear for this wonderful gift, maybe this is why you came into my life.

I hope that by now you know that I believe the world is connected in magical ways. Stella, you were my magic when I needed magic more than ever in my life.

Momma thanking me...I couldn't read any more... my tears were blinding, and my heart hurt; I could hardly breathe. Momma, what are you talking about...me magic? My superpowers failed you. You're wrong...and I'm sorry. I should have left the letter sealed in that beautiful envelope. This was a terrible mistake.

I found myself storming up to my bedroom, placing the envelope in my drawer and climbing into bed. Following close behind were Elizabeth, Rosalind, William, and Paul. I guess I made more noise than I realized. They gathered around me—all having had similar reactions the first time they read their letters. "We struggled to get through them and cried bitterly afterward," William explained.

Oh! So this is why they never talked to me about their letters. It isn't that they didn't want to; they couldn't.

"It took us a long time, Stella, until we could talk about our reactions. We still have not shared our letters with each other." William did most of the talking. Everyone else nodded in agreement. It was Elizabeth and Rosalind who sat practically on top of me, holding me so tight that I thought I would suffocate.

Finally, my tears subsided, and my sisters let loose. Paul suggested that we all go downstairs, pop some popcorn, and make hot chocolate. "Sounds good to me," I whispered. I had about enough for one night.

I am not sure when I will feel ready to finish Momma's letter. For now, high school is getting ready to start. I am busy buying clothes and supplies, and getting my room ready. Momma's letter is in my drawer, and sometimes I just hold it. For now, this is enough.

Age Sixteen

Momma's Letter Revisited

I have finally turned sixteen, and decided it is time to read the rest of Momma's letter. Until now, I would take it out of my drawer, hold it, look at it, and smell it, but never read it. I knew there was so much more to read, but I didn't feel ready. Also, high school has been an extremely busy time. My workload has been over the top, and my school activities fill in all of the other waking hours. On the home front, my sisters and brothers have carried on as usual; nothing really seemed to change during these past few years.

So, you ask, why now? Well, you see, it is time for me to drive. To my surprise, Momma's car has been saved for me. My sisters and brothers fixed it up with fresh paint and shiny new wheels. I am in love. Of course, they are making me take a mechanic's course so that I can learn how to change the oil and a flat tire. My brothers keep reminding me that no sister of theirs will ever be accused of being helpless.

This feels like the right time to read Momma's letter from start to finish. If my siblings are going to entrust me with Momma's car, I need to be strong enough to hear her voice. At some level, I also yearn for her parenting—the kind I imagine the others were lucky to have experienced. It makes no difference to me if it is scolding or tough; I just want it— I need it, like you need a coat in the cold. I need to wrap Momma's words around me before I get behind the wheel of the car she spent so much time in, and especially before I am the driver looking over at the seat that I used to sit in when she drove. I picture her giving me driving lessons—but the reality is—she didn't teach any of the kids to drive. My sisters and brothers went to driving school. It was Poppa who braved the world with each new driver in the family. He is older now, but still willing to take his life in his hands for me. And of course, Paul teases me, but also makes time for me to practice. He has truly taken his place in the family. We are five extraordinarily close siblings.

I decided to read Momma's letter in my room. No hoopla this time, just Momma and me.

To my darling daughter Stella,

Words cannot express how much I love you. After years of not expecting to have any more children, you entered my life, happy, busy, cheerful, and talkative, with so much to say. I think this is what I enjoy most about you. Stella, you have so many amazing qualities. I admire how much you think and care about things, always wanting answers, and always asking questions. I know that your sisters and brothers get annoyed at times, but don't stop! Being inquisitive and curious will get you far in this lifetime.

Stella, an aura of magnetism surrounds you. Since you were a little girl, people have been drawn to you. You are what they call a showstopper. These qualities will also get you far in life.

Your letter is the hardest one for me to write. By now, I am sure you know that I have written to all of your sisters and brothers. You are so young, and there are so many things we didn't get to talk about. I will try to give you as many of my thoughts and wishes as I can in this letter. Your sisters and brothers have so much to offer you; I trust that they will fill in for me.

You are very fortunate to have grown sisters and brothers to share your life with. I can't imagine how I can possibly write, in this small space, everything I need and want you to know, all of life's lessons and all of my thoughts and wishes. Thankfully, Elizabeth, Rosalind, and William have heard enough from me over the years that there isn't too much they can't recite by heart.

I feel a bit lost as to how to begin to guide and parent you through life with only some short words and paragraphs. My heart aches for all of your firsts that I will miss. I will mostly miss seeing you smile when you are happy and holding you when you are sad. I am so grateful that you have two wonderful women, Elizabeth and Rosalind, to do this for you. They love you dearly.

I had to think long and hard about all of the wishes and dreams I have for you, just especially for you, Stella. Even though you are one of five, you are unique. All during my illness (our illness), you had a way of bringing everyone together, keeping the family busy with daily routines, and keeping the family at home.

Everyone, especially me, benefited from the family spending so much time at home. Since I was housebound for such a long period of time, it was comforting to have all of my kids around. The hustle and bustle of activity helped me a great deal and kept a smile on my face. I loved hearing the music, the sounds of clanking in the kitchen, and the sound of your voice telling stories and jokes.

You see, Stella, without you, the older kids might have spent more time at school or work, and in general, doing things outside of the house. Because of you, there was a good reason to be home. Because of you, everyone was busy with kid stuff and found lots of reasons to laugh. Thank you my dear for this wonderful gift, maybe this is why you came into my life.

I hope that by now you know that I believe the world is connected in magical ways. Stella, you were my magic when I needed magic more than ever in my life.

Stella, I tried to figure out the best way to write this letter and decided that an interview, my imagined interview with you, was the perfect solution. Stella, this is our interview, the interview that I imagine would happen, if you could ask me questions about life.

Stella: Momma, since you are not here, how am I supposed to know what to do and what is important?

Momma: Stella, one of the jobs of parenting is guiding your children through life. In the midst of all the fun, there is the sense of obligation to one's children, to direct them and help them set up successful paths to the future. It is the same in every species—the mother gets her children ready for the outside world, a world in which you will find yourself, a world in which I will not be able to protect you, a world in which you will have to be able to depend on yourself. Of course, there will always be a sister or brother around for support. But, Stella, there will be challenges and times that you will be on your own. There will be choices and decisions that no one but you can make. I will try to guide you through with some words of wisdom, some words of plain parental stuff (what good would all of this do if I didn't give you some good old-fashioned parenting), and some words of wishes and hope.

Do your best in school and excel in something. Find your favorite subject and embrace it. Education is truly the key to your future. This is the single most important thing you can do that will change the course of your life forever. Being educated is the most important single gift I wish for you.

Always stay connected to your family, especially your sisters and brothers. No matter what course life takes you on, talk to them often, and stay involved in their lives. This is the one thing that will ensure your sense of well-being. Life is empty without these connections. Life is empty without people to love and share it with. These relationships are as important as the air you breathe; love and nurture them.

Listen to your sisters and brothers. Do your chores and behave yourself. They are now your parents. Mind them and follow their advice. Their word is my word. Their kisses and hugs are mine too.

Be a good friend. A good friend is someone that you can count on, someone that keeps your secrets and helps you when you are in trouble, someone to have fun with, and last but not least, someone you can laugh and cry with.

Get ready for Mommy-isms.

Shower or bath every day and change your clothes. You are going to become a young lady soon, and you need to be clean and smell good.

When you want to date, talk to the older ones. William will be good at telling you how a boy should treat you.

Don't be afraid to defend yourself. Be wary of strangers. The world is not as safe as it used to be.

Don't ever let anyone tell you that you can't accomplish something. You can do whatever you set your mind on.

Have fun and play. Take time to do fun things.

Have adventures. Don't be afraid to try new things. It doesn't matter if you are not great at everything. Have experiences.

Be part of the community—volunteer, vote, read the newspaper, and stay informed.

There are probably a million more, but most importantly, I want to talk to you about how I feel. Stella, I am so sorry that I got sick and could not be the kind of mom I wanted to be for you or the kind of mom you deserve. You may not understand right now, but I will always be in your heart. I know that your sisters and brothers love you very much and will take good care of you. They are great people; we are all fortunate for that gift.

Although I am not there, I trust and expect that you will do your best to make me proud; it gives me comfort to know that you will. My darling little Stella, you are the dream and glory of my life. I wish you all of the happiness, success, and health a person can have.

Now I have a very special request of you. Please promise, me…that's right, right now, say, "I promise you, Momma."

Promise me that you will always rely on your sisters and brothers. That you will go to them for advice, for help when you are in trouble, to help you problem solve any dilemma that comes your way, to pick you up when you fall, and to cheer when you rally. This will not make you dependent on them, but it will allow you to lean on them. The strength of the family can help you through any challenge that comes your way.

Promise me that you will be brave and strong. I know you will be very sad when I die. It would break my heart to think that my death interfered with you doing in life what you love. Being brave and strong means living, doing, achieving, loving, and enjoying through the pain and hard times.

Promise me that when you are older you will read about Christopher Reeve. He is my hero. He lived a charmed life, and then had an accident that changed everything. He learned to live life under some of life's most difficult challenges. He said, "I think a hero is an ordinary individual who finds the strength to persevere and endure in spite of overwhelming obstacles." We are these ordinary people. We are these heroes. He should be a role model for everyone.

Life is so much more than what we experience at any particular moment in time. I don't think we have any idea, or can possibly grasp, how wonderful and mysterious the world is and how we are all connected in life and what we call afterlife. I wish I had better answers for you about religion and God, but I do not. These larger questions are yet for you to discover, ponder and find some answers, or become comfortable with not finding the answer.

What I do know is that I believe in people, in relationships, and in the power of love. I believe in education and living a deliberate thought-about life. Not just letting life take you along for the ride, but participating in life and accepting responsibility for how you respond to whatever situations life offers. I believe in dedication to relationships and oneself.

Whatever you are involved with, take care of it, nurture it, and love it. We only have one life, Stella; I want you to be proud of yourself and satisfied with it. I have been with mine.

I have loved being your mom. My children, our family, have truly been my greatest pleasure and joy. It certainly hasn't hurt that all of you are so smart and charming.

I have enjoyed my career, and feel confident that my participation in the school district has made a contribution to the academic world and to all of the children whose lives I touched.

Whenever you need to be close to me, just think about me, and I will be thinking about you. Close your eyes…and

I will comfort you. Look up at the stars…and I will shine down on you. Look at my picture…and I will smile back.

Please take care of yourself and remember, always, how much I love you.

Forever yours, Momma

For a long while I just sat and stared at the letter. It was as if I couldn't quite get a grip on what I had read. It was not what I expected. What did I expect? I don't know. Maybe this is the kind of thing that grows on you as you get older.

Then, all of a sudden, tears started pouring down my face. Strange strong feelings of hurt and anger swelled up inside of me. I wanted to scream…but couldn't. My mind kept repeating—it isn't fair that I should have to be a hero—I don't want to be a hero—I just want my Momma and my ordinary life back. My momma should have known that it wasn't fair to expect me to be OK.

Paul must have heard me and came into my room. When he saw how distressed I was, he pulled me downstairs and outside, all the while calling for everyone to join us. Almost as one voice, they asked, "Are you OK, Stella?" My head was in my hands, and I was hysterical.

"No," I shouted, " I am not and never will be. Now go away and leave me alone." The four of them, these big people, surrounded me, saying, "Let's scream." All together they began to scream, yelling over and over, "It's not fair…it's not fair."

Before I knew it, they were all on the ground pounding their fists and yelling. I am not sure how I got on the ground, but I was screaming and pounding too. Then, slowly, one by one, we stopped; what a site—the five of us lying on the ground just panting. Eventually, we went inside, made hot chocolate, and cuddled in the living room. There was no need for talk. Someone turned on the music, Momma's music, and we just sat until we fell asleep.

In the morning, we got up and started our day as usual. During dinner, Paul proposed that we should make time for more screaming and pounding episodes. He said he hadn't realized how much he needed that release, and how much better he felt afterward. Paul sharing an emotion, wow, everyone laughed and agreed.

I placed Momma's letter in my nightstand; every now and then I take it out to hold. Rosalind tells me that as I get older, I will find lots of comfort in reading it. For now, just holding it is fine for me.

Oh, yes, Elizabeth showed me the beautiful necklace that awaits me on my eighteenth birthday. To hold me over, my siblings presented me with a special necklace from them. They decided that since I couldn't have Momma's until I was eighteen and they were my surrogates, I could have one from them instead. So I wear my beautiful necklace of intertwining circles day and night. I never take it off, not even when swimming.

I should probably end with some thoughts of my own. Most interviews end with the interviewer summarizing the interview. I'd say that as a family, this is a pretty good one. We have survived one of life's most difficult challenges. It looks like the pain of losing Momma will be with all of us forever. I don't think you ever get used to your mom dying. I think you just get used to living without her. And if you are lucky like me, you have sisters and brothers or someone to love and take care of you. This is now our family, complete and whole, except for fulfilling life the way Momma wished for.

Age Eighteen

Having just turned eighteen, I once again find myself analyzing my life's journey. I had not realized and certainly could not have predicted, at ages thirteen or sixteen, that I would want and have the need to revisit my family's interviews or that new questions would arise for me. I guess this is becoming a habit, or should I say ritual, or as they say in introductory psychology, a rite of passage.

Developmental issues are interesting for me. I have searched and searched in my attempts to read about children who experience the death of a parent and how their development is impacted. Well, as you can probably guess, I think I will major in psychology in college.

These interviews have become more than just a way to manage my mother's death; they have become my life's work. I can foresee that my entire life's development will be evaluated through this lens. Hopefully, my ability to write about my life will help other children, teens, and young adults through their parental losses.

It has become clear to me that by losing my Momma so early in life, I never had the chance to really know her. I have no idea what her faults were, and I certainly never had the opportunity to be mad or angry at her about life stuff. We never had the chance to argue about curfew, or chores, or sloppy rooms, like my friends have with their moms.

Somehow, in my momma's shadow, I had to be more responsible and more grown-up. I became part of the family with my sisters and brothers rather early. In retrospect, this is not a bad thing. After all, what does all that conflict get you anyway? But still, the normalcy of it sounds good. I wonder if my experience parallels that of kids during the depression or in wartime. I recently saw a documentary about kids in one the poorest towns in Africa. These kids, whose parents had been killed or died from illnesses, were like me. They had to take care of each other and the town. They became adults before their time.

Maybe ordinary childhood isn't everything it is cracked up to be. I look at my friends' lives and recognize that they are really no happier or content than I am. Their complaints and unrest are about relatively small things— boys liking them, hairdos, clothes, and staying out late. These things are important to me, but on a scale of one to ten, about a three, and certainly not important enough to make it difficult on my sisters and brothers. I think this is called having a conscience. It is, however, a mixed bag. I am sorry that these small things are not a bigger deal to me. I am not sorry that I don't get in trouble or have conflicts with my surrogate parents. But not knowing the freedom of the other side stops me in my tracks.

I bet you are wondering what the rest of the family has been up to during these years. Let me fill you in. It has been seven years since my mother's death, and I think we are just starting to recover. We have maintained a fairly uneventful life. Everyone has remained at home, focusing on his or her careers and basically my life and me. My siblings were determined to make sure that I did not miss out on anything. It has been, and continues to be, the fulfillment of an unspoken commitment and promise to Momma. Our house is usually a flurry of activity, focused around my friends and me. Dinners continue to be a grand event, and all of Momma's rituals continue as well.

Nana and Poppa are still alive, getting old gracefully and yet requiring assistance from all of us. William continues to live there, which has enabled them to remain in their home. When he is not at Nana and Poppa's, he is at his lab or at our house.

Elizabeth is engaged to a warm and amazing man. Who would have thought? She is marrying another journalist, and they are talking about traveling the world and gathering human-interest stories. They don't really talk about starting a family of their own... maybe she has already had her family.

Rosalind has a serious boyfriend. She is not sure that marriage is right for her. Although she has taken over much of the household responsibilities, she continues to spend a great deal of time on her research and teaching. As life has it, she did not become an astronaut, but she is a well-respected leader in the research field of space travel. Despite many opportunities to lecture all across the country, she has not yet taken advantage of them...I am sure that she will now.

Surprise of surprises, Paul has no plans to move out. He studied engineering, and now works for our county in housing development. He is very social, has many friends, and remains popular with the women. I am sure that some day he will run for mayor.

I think my graduating from high school and leaving for college has brought a new sense of freedom to my family. Maybe Paul was right about everyone staying home to maintain a normal life for me. I will be the first one in the family to leave. I decided to go away to school. It felt like the right time for me to have other experiences. After reading Momma's letter, for only the millionth time, I decided to start having adventures. This is my first. This also seems like an ideal time to once again interview my sisters and brothers. But life is so hectic with Elizabeth's wedding and my graduation...I think these interviews will have to wait.

Age Twenty-One

W here and how do I begin? This feels so familiar and yet so foreign. It has been three years since I last looked at my interviews and read them through from beginning to end. I am amazed and deeply moved at how thoughtful and heartfelt my writings are. There are brilliant spots of sadness combined with warm and charming parts of connectedness.

What I find most surprising…though I am sure you will not be surprised…is how similar this twenty-one-year-old woman is to that eight-year-old girl.

It is the summer before my senior year at college. I have just turned twenty-one, which means I have officially entered adulthood. Yet I don't feel any different. My sisters keep telling me not to rush things. Getting older, they say, creeps up on you. One minute you are young, and the next you are old, not realizing when it happened and certainly unable to identify where all of the time has gone. As the saying goes, life is not a dress rehearsal, and it certainly doesn't last forever. As a family, we know this truth intimately. Losing our mom brought this reality to us sooner than most.

My college major, as it turns out, is philosophy and not journalism or psychology. I realized that I loved being part of the debate, part of the action, and an active part of the conversation. These qualities combined with my passionate and emotional response set— are not exactly successful interviewer traits. So here I am, age twenty-one, and still talking all of the time. Some things never change.

The impetus for exploring my earlier writings was born out of necessity of having to produce a senior project. In order to graduate, the philosophy department, being what it is, requires its students to create an original piece of work. In thinking this through and after much internal debate—after all, I am a philosophy major, and debating with one's own thoughts is a requirement—I decided to do my project on "The meaning of life as found in one's family." Throughout the centuries, people have pondered the meaning of life. In many writings, the meaning of life takes on a very abstract, esoteric, global approach. I am interested in the more usual, everyday meaning that people define for themselves. I guess I haven't moved that far away from my human-interest roots. I can thank Elizabeth for this.

My life plan is to continue my education in graduate school and become a professor. As always, I have found a creative way to use my love of thoughts and words. I experimented with many different avenues of expression—acting classes, working for the school airwaves as a news broadcaster, and working for the school newspaper as a reporter. Out of desperation, I went as far as trying a standup comedy class. Unfortunately, even though I pride myself on my sense of humor, I'm definitely too serious. I like to have as much fun as the next person, but I love the intellectual heady stuff. What can I say? Philosophy floats my boat…so philosophy it is!

In rereading my interviews, our history, and my family's journey surrounding my mother's illness and death, I realized that my life has been tinted with a layer of seriousness that most young people are not exposed to. My mother's illness and death overwhelmed my family with the realities of life. As a family, we lost the naïve sense of forever. I never did develop the adolescent sense of "it will never happen to me." At an early age, I learned that life can be devastating, and yet you go on breathing. Life can challenge everything you ever thought of as true and safe. Life can challenge your very will and desire to live. Life can be so painful that you are not sure you can take another step. In this look back, it is painfully clear how: as a family we just pushed through, how many questions I now have, all of the many conversations with my mother that did not happen, just how left out I was at eight and eleven and thirteen, how much I don't know about how my sisters and brothers managed their pain, and how much anger I would still have at twenty-one.

My mother is a mystery to me. Although I have memories and pictures, I don't feel like I know her. I wonder how different I might feel if my mother had talked to me about what was happening—if she could have anticipated how much I would need her at twenty-one— if I would feel more satisfied, more complete. I am not sure that feeling complete is anything I will ever experience. There is a part of me gone forever.

Wow, I'm really angry. I had no idea that I was holding onto so much anger. My friends and teachers would be shocked. I seem great. I thought I was great. Maybe being angry is not counterproductive to being great. Maybe they can coexist, not like in harmony, but just side by side. Maybe this is one of the challenges you face when your mother dies during your childhood. Of course, I imagine it is similar if you lose a father, but I don't know that. In my future studies, I am sure this will be part of my research. Modern day philosophy allows for reflecting on the past and future. It allows me to look at the larger picture from a small focal point, and apply the vast world of meaning to life in many forms.

Depressed, unhappy, you ask? No, I am not. I have had a wonderful time in college. The dorms were noisy and busy, just like my house. In fact, I think I adjusted better than most. I was accustomed to doing chores, being busy, and living with lots of commotion. What I missed and craved was the warmth and caring of my sisters and brothers. Our phone bill was out of control at first and then calmed down. They continue to be very involved parents; they have never made the transition to siblings. I have four parents, each with their own strong opinions and ideas.

No, this has not been easy. Each of them held expectations for my career. I have done a great service to any children that will follow in this family. I have sufficiently covered any first child syndromes one can imagine. Children...now, that is an interesting topic. So far my siblings have not presented me with a niece or nephew. Our mother's illness and death has had a profound effect on all of us.

My senior project offers me the opportunity to have new conversations with my siblings. I no longer have the childish need to do an interview. I no longer need to hide behind the interview. I now have the need to discuss, to understand, and to share my feelings and hear theirs.

Sadly, the one person I yearn to talk to is not here. If only I could...for just one time...and then...all I would probably do is cry in her arms.

As you can well imagine, my family was delighted to have me home for the summer. For the last two summers, I have stayed at school, taking classes and working on projects involving different school activities. I have been so immersed in school that it is hard to believe my senior year has arrived. College has been a wonderful time for me. I knew that it would not go on forever, but thinking about it ending never crossed my mind. I just enjoyed every day. What about home you ask? I have not been avoiding home. I was home for every holiday and family function. There were times when I was home so often that it felt as if I had never left. However, this is the first time I will be home for a solid three months. This project is my only true responsibility. Of course, I will help around the house and fit right back into the scheduled chores, but I do not have any other pressing responsibilities. This is the most amount of freedom I have ever experienced—waking up each day and deciding what I feel like doing, what a concept.

The house hasn't changed all that much. Rosalind, William, and Paul still officially live there. Rosalind travels and is hardly home. William spends most of his time at the lab and at Nana and Poppa's. My grandparents have lived long healthy lives thanks to my siblings, especially William. William's dedication as the family caregiver is at this point grounded in concrete. Elizabeth and her husband have their own place. Sunday dinners continue to be the center of our family's traditions. When Rosalind is traveling, she calls on a Webcam and eats her meal with us. Sundays are the best part of being home, and what I missed the most when I was away. At college, I also had a

Webcam and ate with the family, but it was not the same. In fact, oftentimes it left me missing them more than ever. Some of my friends thought that it was a bit weird, our Sunday traditions. I never did. The comfort and reassurance of their connection kept me strong and focused.

I bet you want to know about the necklace my mom left. It is a beautiful silver and gold antique heart on a delicate, yet sturdy, chain. The inscription on the back is simple: *Forever Yours, Momma*. As you might have guessed, I also wear the necklace that my sisters and brothers gave me. So I carry my family with me everywhere. You might think that all of this family would make up for my mom. It doesn't. Yes, the house does not feel empty anymore, but her lack of presence in our lives is noticed daily—sometimes on and off all day long. It is clear to me that just because someone dies, they are not really gone. They are just gone from sight and touch.

I decided to organize my project around a series of family roundtables. A bit of the journalist still lives on in me. As a family, we decided to have these roundtables on the Sundays that Rosalind is home and after dinner in the backyard. Of course, Rosalind made a special effort to be home more this summer than she had in years.

Surprisingly, my family seemed excited at the prospects of having a philosophical discussion about life. In the past interviews, I felt as if my family would have done everything and anything to help me with my grief. This time it feels different. This time it feels more communal. This time it is about each of us, as well as our mom. This time it is about a group of people who love and adore each other, discussing life in a very deep and meaningful way. This time it feels like the truth.

Sitting across from my siblings during our first evening roundtable, I realized how different and similar we are. They were closer to my age now when our mother died. I finally feel as if I have caught up to them.

I was excited and a bit nervous about starting. Before I realized what was happening, I started hyperventilating. I felt just like that little eleven-year-old girl as she listened to William whisper the bad news about our mother. All I could think about was running away…sound familiar? The last two times I tried to do something formal like this, I was blown out of the water, emotionally overwhelmed, and unable to continue. I thought I had outgrown that response…I guess not.

Faced with this challenge, I instinctually knew that I was not alone. I envisioned others like Elie Wiesel, who found the strength to write and talk about the trauma of living through the holocaust while his entire family was exterminated; the enormous pain, fear, and anguish that he endured and his ability to manage his emotions in face of reliving his heartache. Don't misunderstand; I am not suggesting that my mother's death and his experience in a concentration camp were the same. I am seeking, yearning, searching to find strength in the midst of my pain. I turn to Christopher Reeve's writings. I look and search for how others lived through and with their pain. Now I am looking closer to home. I know it will be more emotional hearing from my sisters and brothers. After all, their pain is my pain, not just empathy pain, but gut-level, heart-throbbing pain. I took a deep breath and decided to start the roundtable by talking about college—what it was like as a philosophy major, being away from home, and feeling connected yet disconnected from my peers. A true existential dilemma I attributed to my mother's death.

William was the first to speak, "Stella, as I sit here listening to you, I can't help but reflect on how my life has been all about our mom's illness and death." He continued, "My science career could have taken many roads but ended up with Momma's disease as its dictator. I feel compelled to participate in finding a cure for cancer. The ultimate meaning of my life is in my work and its accomplishments."

OK, the heat was on. Elizabeth practically jumped out of her chair. "William, I knew you were passionate about your work, but I had no idea that you were so exclusive about your life. Does it mean that you give up everything else for this one meaning, that you will never have an intimate relationship, that your family takes second or third place? What if you don't find a cure for cancer—will your life have been futile?"

William thoughtfully responded, "I really don't know how to answer."

Rosalind softly and gently asked William, "Surely you must value the way in which you helped Mom at the worst time in her life. William, do you find any comfort in knowing that you were her strength, the one person she counted on to help her, the one person that was truly able to comfort her mind and soul?"

William answered, "Of course, I felt privileged to have been able to support Mom, but I was unable to do the one thing she really needed, save her life. Now I know that sounds ridiculous, but it is how I feel. If I can save lives, I can earn some sense of vindication."

The group fell silent.

Paul looked up with an intense sincerity in his eyes and began to talk. "William, I can't begin to tell you what meaning you have brought to my life. You are the only adult male I have ever relied on. You have been my stability and strength. When Mom was sick, I never worried. I knew that you would take care of her. When she died, I never worried about us as a family. I knew you would take care of us. Until this very moment, I don't think I realized how you had become my dad. Even though I was six when Dad left, he wasn't *here* even when he was here. You were always the one I looked up to and looked for. I am not sure how my life would have turned out without you. For me, William, the meaning of life is in our relationships."

Now everyone was crying, and I had not been prepared. I guess my interview instincts have grown cold. I fetched the tissues.

William stayed very still, looking into Paul's eyes as he spoke. "Paul, you know how much I love you. I do feel like your dad/brother…certainly more like a brother the older we get."

William continued, "Elizabeth, I don't think I expressed myself clearly. I find a great sense of meaning and satisfaction in being part of this family." William looked around at each of us as tears rolled down his face. "It has been my pleasure and joy to be the oldest male in the family. In fact, my needs for a family are quite satisfied. I love our Sunday dinners and our talks during the week. I love knowing that I can steal time with any of you whenever I want. Please don't mistake my sense of drive at work, my sense of need to achieve, as my not needing all of you. In fact, you all do such a great job of loving and caring that it allows me the space to dedicate my life to Mom. I hope you can understand this and continue to support my work and my life."

As a group, as if on cue, we shook our heads and whispered yes.

At this point, I was the only one (in addition to Elizabeth's husband Sam, whose participation wasn't expected) who had not replied in some fashion to William. I looked up at William and told him that I felt a similar sense of obligation to Momma.

"Until this summer," I said, "I had not appreciated how her death had steered my education and career choice… that my need to explore the meaning of life is all wrapped up in her illness and death."

As I looked around at my siblings, I talked openly and honestly for the first time about my needs. My voice started low and got louder and louder as I questioned them. How on earth did Momma not realize that I needed her to talk to me? How could she have so underestimated my need to have her guide me through her illness and inevitable death? Did she really think that a letter would do? Did she really think that anyone else would do? Did she really not understand that even though all of you love me dearly, I needed her to be my parent, my guide, and that it was her voice I needed to hear? Now I was angry, not crying... just plain mad. It continued to pour out of me, streams and streams of wants, needs, and hurts. It seemed to me that Momma abandoned her basic teachings about connected-ness, about responsibility, about how much she loved us, and ended up doing what was comfortable for her. There, I said it, all of the thoughts that were for so long locked away inside of me.

Elizabeth, in a much calmer manner, looked me straight in the eye and said, "Stella, I disagree completely. Our mother never did anything without thoughtful con-sideration and in-depth discussion. In fact, we talked and talked and talked, until we agreed upon how much infor-mation we would share with you. What we didn't realize was that at eight or nine or eleven years, your needs were exactly the same as ours. Stella, it was a lack of knowl-edge, a lack of understanding, and a lack of guidance. Not once did a doctor, neighbor, or relative suggest that we get help for you and Paul. No one advised us about how to handle Momma's illness or death. Not one person said, 'The kids have special needs. Let me help you with them.' Our own grief and worry was so overwhelming that we could not have possibly thought of everything ourselves. Stella, I am so sorry that we did not know what to do. I was consumed by my responsibilities of taking care of Momma and keeping things going on as usual. During Momma's illness, it took every ounce of energy just keep-ing up with the daily demands of life. If I stopped for even a moment, I'd cry and grieve. My solution was to keep moving. In reflecting back, it seems as if I made a conscious decision not to feel anything. I haven't talked about this with anyone…sorry, Sam, not even you. I was angry during Momma's illness, angry at the cancer, angry with Momma for leaving me with the family, angry with Dad for deserting us, angry at life. I was a caregiver my entire youth, and it felt like I was destined forever to maintain that role."

Elizabeth, shocked at her own words, gasped, "I can't believe I said that. I love all of you. I love being your sister…I just miss Momma…I miss the safety of having a mom. I miss having the one person you know is always going to be there with love and support. Rosalind, William, Paul, and Stella, I know you love me and will always be there, but you also know what I am talking about. Having a mom offers the kind of stability you can't find anywhere else." As Elizabeth talked, she calmed down.

We knew she was right because we all felt the same way. We also knew that we had become each other's stability. We knew that through our rituals, we had kept Momma alive within our circle. We also knew that if we didn't talk about her or include her in our circle, she would still have her place there. Trying to tell the truth, while watching out for each other's feelings, was not an easy task. This exploration was more intense than any of us had anticipated. Yet we hung in there. It was as if we had finally given ourselves permission to share our deepest, darkest thoughts. It was as if our love and security allowed us to face, together, the enormous emotional pain and suffering we had for so long been alone with. Even in our close-knit family, these most intimate and private thoughts had been kept secret.

I asked, "Why do you imagine that we have not been having these types of family discussions before now?"

William answered, "Stella, do you remember the book you gave me to read about kids and grief?"

I replied, "Of course."

William continued, "In preparing for this meeting, I took another look at the book. Do you remember about the timeline?"

I laughed, "Yes, I remember."

William continued, "The timeline talked about grief as an on-going process, a continuum. If you remember, Stella, kids who had a parent that died wrote the book. Missing your parent never goes away. As your life progresses, the desire to share it with your parent is the one constant you can count on. The kids described the pain of this loss as moving from a sharp knife in your heart to a dull pain. It is a pain that at times you don't even notice unless you are reminded of it. However, it is always there, lingering in the background, easy to access, and not far below the surface."

Rosalind chimed in, "Oh boy is that ever so true! I think about Momma all the time. For the most part, they are joyous thoughts. At night, I still look at the stars and talk to her. In fact, I probably talk to her several times a week. I never feel too far from her no matter where I am. I think this is because of how at peace Momma was with her life. She never complained. All during her illness, she talked about the wonderment of life's journey. She was convinced about our connectedness to each other and the mystical way we live on forever in our relationships. For me, she was the perfect example of self-actualization. Don't take this wrong, Stella. I am not discounting what you needed or the fact that Momma and all of us missed that. If you look at Momma's life, just through Momma's eyes, she was satisfied. Of course, she wasn't perfect and would have loved to live to a ripe old age. But she was pleased with how she handled life and all of its twists, turns, and surprises. When faced with difficult situations, she thought them through and made a conscious decision about how to handle them. Unfortunately, those decisions have not always been complete or the best. But she tried, and when she realized that her choices weren't working out, she changed course. She never showed her fear. She did what she had to do and definitely enjoyed her freedom and independence. She prided herself on her family and ultimately found her greatest joy in our relationships. She used to tell me that being at home with us kids was the best part of her day. As much as she enjoyed her work, friends, parents, and other relatives, it was us that she relished in. Since she had become a parent at such a young age, she was surprised at how much she enjoyed us. She would look around and see how difficult it was for women to enjoy their families. She never felt that way. In part, Elizabeth and William helped in that arena. Momma always talked about how the two of you became her partners in addition to her children. She would describe how this just came about naturally, everyone helping and participating in the family operations. She was proud of us as a team."

Rosalind continued, "Elizabeth, I never told you how truly sad I was when you were getting married. Not sad that you were getting married, but sad that I was not Momma. I worried obsessively about every finite detail. I didn't want Momma's absence to overshadow your joy and happiness. I wanted your wedding to be everything you ever dreamed of. I wanted your wedding to be perfect."

"Rosalind, because of you it was perfect," Elizabeth replied, "but missing Momma…that was inevitable and unavoidable. If you remember, we cried about it just before the wedding. Even with Momma's absence, I never felt like anything was missing. You did everything and more for me, and I love you. "

Elizabeth continued, "Rosalind, I agree with your assessment of Momma. She never asked for help. She never made demands about needing help. It was unspoken. My job was to team with her and William, and that was just how it was."

Paul added, "Maybe it grew out of how Momma thought about us. Our house was always a bit different than my friends'. I used to think it was because there were so many adults living together. But now I think it was because of Momma's attitude. She respected and enjoyed us. Her perception of us as a team permeated our lifestyle. There were no divisions even though there were clear rules and expectations. I knew that I was expected to get good grades, and I did. But I don't ever remember Momma checking up on me to see if my work was completed." Elizabeth, William, and Rosalind all broke out in laughter; we remembered well the un-pressure pressure, one of mom's unique parenting tools.

William continued, "Momma had an uncanny way of letting you know what was to happen—she expected it and got it. If we could bottle and sell this, we'd all be wealthy."

The pieces were starting to fit together for me.

I joined in, "This is probably why Momma could not anticipate what her death would do to me, to us. She did not really know about feeling unstable. Her world was rock solid, and therefore, she had no concept of how her death would rock our family. She just assumed we would handle things the way she always did. The missing piece, for Momma, was in her lack of having experienced a life event that even came close to the emotional impact that her death has had on us. Whoever said ignorance is bliss was lying. Well, maybe for Momma it was bliss, thinking we'd be fine. For us, the recipients of that bliss, the end result has not been gratifying."

By this time, we realized how late it was; the moon was shining brightly and the stars were sparkling. We were spent and tired, and decided as our family does, to have some dessert and call it a night.

I was very interested in the new family member, Sam, and his reaction to this family exchange. When I asked him what he thought, he said he wasn't the least bit surprised. He said that one of the things he fell in love with when he met Elizabeth was the family. He knew that he didn't just marry a woman; he married a family, and not just your run of the mill family, but a family he could call his own, a family that anyone would be lucky to be a part of, a family that he hoped to cherish forever. "My one regret," he said, "is that I will never meet your mother."

I said, "You are wrong on that account. Just look closely. You can see her in all of us."

Final Chapter

I have spent the past month relaxing, reading, working on this project, and awaiting the next roundtable. This time away from school has been good for me. It has afforded me time to visit friends and relatives, and time to just sit out back, under a tree, reconnecting to my life as never before. This is truly my life, my place of safety, stability, and comfort—a place I can stay at forever. Thinking about returning to school feels like an intrusion. I can't remember the last time I felt so comfortable and content. I finally understand why nobody left—why William, Rosalind, and Paul continue to live in our house. I finally understand why my sisters and brothers seem satisfied with the lives they are living.

I started the second and last of our meetings exploring the issue of contentment. I shared my newly discovered revelations, and wondered if my assessment of their choices was correct.

Paul started by saying that he was excited and very content in his life. He talked about how he never thought he'd find a place of peace, how his teen years were difficult, how his avoidance of the family was the only way he could survive Momma's illness, and how for years he felt enormous amounts of guilt and shame that he had dishonored his mother and his family by hiding. He shared about his late night visits to Momma and how hard he tried to avoid seeing her, and how impossible it was to fall asleep until he did. "For me," he said, "the internal pressure to see Momma and talk to her overrode my fear, sadness, and grief at seeing her so frail and ill. Eventually, I came to understand that teenage boy and forgave him."

Paul continued to tell us that his sense of calm, peace, and contentment is found in his work, friends, family, and this house. Waking up every day and going to sleep every night in this marvelous place of safety, stability, and memories allows for the rest of his life to be as good as it is.

Rosalind laughed, "Paul that was very well stated. I don't think I could have put it in such perfect terms. I have always thought that I felt this way because of my travels. When I get home, I feel as if I can breathe again. I had not recognized that my connection and sense of relief was much deeper and fundamental."

"This is very interesting," Elizabeth said. "I have managed to move out with relatively no ambivalence. Maybe it is because I am here so often, or maybe it is because all of you are still here and things have remained unchanged…or maybe it is because I felt the need for change. Prior to our last roundtable meeting, I don't think I appreciated how strong my need for self-identity had grown. Amongst all of us, my identity was the one most connected to Momma. I was, and felt like, her shadow, her right hand, and her confidant. I don't think Momma planned it that way, but it was how it turned out. The only way I could live and tolerate her loss was to have some distance from the family, not distance in our relationships, just my own address. It's funny, but I love being here at the house. I am so happy when I am here, and I love being with all of you. In fact, I rarely desire to be anywhere else, except my own home."

"Elizabeth," I asked, "what about kids? Do you ever think of having any?"

Elizabeth, in a soft whisper, answered, "Sam and I have had long talks about having children. This family has so completely filled my need for children that I have never experienced any cravings for a baby, as my friends have. After all, at any given time, I have had two or four children to watch over, care for, and protect. However, I think about the family and how nice it would be for everyone to have children running around the house. I also think about Sam. Yes, Sam…I do think about your needs and desires. I think having children is definitely in our future. However, for this to work, I need help and tons of it. Everyone will have diaper and babysitting duties. For me, staying home full time is not something I feel capable of handling. I am putting all of you on notice—when the time comes, be prepared to work. After all, nothing in this family is off limits to group participation. My children will be your children."

William laughed out loud and squirmed. "Actually," he said, "our last meeting stirred my thoughts and challenged me to rethink my stance on life. After serious consideration, I want you to know that I am very content doing research. I have spent hours thinking about our roundtable and can't find any reason or desire to change my life's course. In fact, I am so compelled to do my work that I can't envision my life any differently."

Rosalind joined in. "I have also found myself replaying our roundtable, rethinking our past and my life decisions. In retrospect, I can see how I floated through Momma's illness. Paul, I think I hid in a different way. I was present and absent at the same time. When I am traveling and alone in some hotel room, I often find myself thinking about Momma when she was ill. It is hard to believe how sick she must have felt and even harder to remember how sick she looked. It was almost unbearable to watch her body fade away into a sickly, almost unrecognizable person. Paul, I wasn't able to tolerate Momma's decline any better than you. I had more responsibility and hid psychologically in Momma's words, philosophy, and ideals about life. When I spent time with her, I saw her but didn't see her, couldn't see her. When I was with Momma, it was as if I was seeing her through my memories, as if I had this beautiful picture of her in my head, and that is the Momma I visited in her room. From time to time, my defenses were weak, and the real Momma would be in front of me. It was these times that I would cry in her arms, unable to contain the enormous amount of heartache that ripped through me. She was always able to comfort me by saying, 'Remember the beauty and remember the great times. Please don't let these times be your lasting memories.'"

At this point, Rosalind was sobbing. Elizabeth was holding her, and the rest of us cried along.

After some time passed, Elizabeth talked about how she had also emotionally hid during our mother's illness. How she stayed distracted by focusing on the family and the never-ending list of chores. She continued, "Rosalind, I am a bit jealous that I never cried with Momma. While taking care of her, helping her dress, bathe, or simply sitting with her, I was numb. I have no recollection of ever having or focusing on a sad feeling during those times with Momma. It wasn't until after her death, months later, when I started missing her presence and started yearning for her company that I became inconsolably sad. The deep depression that crept up on me permeated every part of my body. I thought that I might never feel joy again. What kept me together was having the family to take care of and responsibilities at work. The sadness I felt was so heavy that I was unable to put it into words. Tears were the only means of expressing this uncontrollable emotion. I cried myself to sleep every night for a year. After the second anniversary of her death, I finally found myself able to talk about her. The more I could talk about her, the less I cried at night. Rosalind, do you remember our discussions during this time?"

Rosalind replied, "Of course I do."

Elizabeth continued, "Stella, during this second year, Rosalind and William and I found it easier to talk about Momma. It was as if we were no longer shell-shocked. Words found their way into our conversations in an easier more natural pattern. It was also during this time period that we became increasingly focused and worried about you. You had become withdrawn and sullen. Come to think of it, it was your withdrawal that pulled me out of mine. As usual, you gave us something to focus on other than ourselves. Paul, you continued to be busy and out of the house most of the time. I think we felt you were OK. I had no idea what you were going through. I am so sorry for neglecting you." With this, Elizabeth and Paul simultaneously joined in a hug.

For someone who usually has to break the tension, I found myself without words. My sisters and brothers had so eloquently expressed their shared journey through our mother's illness that there wasn't much else to say.

But, of course, words are never far from my lips, so I started talking. "My dearest sisters and brothers, thank you. As a twenty-one-year-old, I have spent a great deal of time trying to recreate what life was like during those years. It was as if there were pieces of time missing. My experience as that child was far from satisfying. As I have grown through the years, so have the questions, and the desire to have this shared experience with all of you. But after listening to your experience, I can't say I'm sorry that I was eight instead of twenty when Momma was sick. It is clear that my age sheltered me from certain things, but what you all received in return, I will never be able to have…more time with Momma." And so the evening ended with us returning to the kitchen for our comforting ritual of dessert.

Life marched on for our family. I returned to school, finished my senior project, and graduated. The family continued in the same predictable way it had been except for one major change, Elizabeth's pregnancy. Of course, this prompted me to choose a graduate program at our local university. How could I possibly be far away and miss enjoying the new addition to the family? But that was predictable. And of course, Rosalind took a sabbatical from traveling to be with Elizabeth during her pregnancy and to be present for the birth of our niece. Another girl in the family, I guess Elizabeth will just have to have several more children to keep the ratio even. It will be interesting to see if Rosalind decides to resume her travels. We can probably predict the odds of that happening.

As we have learned through the years, my life's journey is far from over.

I will no longer be surprised by my need to revisit the issues surrounding my mother's illness and death at different points in my life. Will I need my family's input again? If I had to guess…I'd probably say "yes." Time will tell.

Author's Note

S tella and her siblings offer us the opportunity to experience, at an intimate level, the loss of a mom. As parents, aunts, uncles, friends, and professionals, we are
not always able to appreciate the deeper inner world of how
parental loss is experienced by children, teens, and young
adults. Self-help books on grief, while they may do a great
job in explaining the process and offer wonderful suggestions
for helping, miss the visceral experience of the children, at all
ages. This can leave supporting adults underestimating what
this experience is truly like for the children.

My hope and desire for you, the reader, is that you
have been on this journey with Stella and her siblings

and not simply as an interested observer, for it is at this complete level of immersion that true healing and help is found. Although no one can ever take this pain away, it is comforting to know that when you look in someone's eyes, there is a genuine understanding. This heartfelt connection is what helps us to be stronger, resilient and lets us know that we are not alone. It is this heartfelt connection that is healing.

I also hope that this story is educational, as to what life is like after the death of a mom. Often, children, teens, and young adults look OK from the outside—they play and continue to thrive in school, vocations, and activities. They often cannot find the words to discuss their loss, even with each other. From the outside, it would be hard to detect the enormous amount of pain they are carrying around inside. From the outside, this pain does not show, and therefore, everyone assumes they are fine, healed, and moving on. The end result is that they are suffering in silence.

For children, teens, and young adults who do not have siblings, for the siblings who cannot get to the point of sharing their emotions, the internal wounds and grief have no avenues in which to be expressed and, therefore, no means to eventually settle down. For some, this can mean a life of unhappiness and unrest, unable to find satisfaction, and left always seeking the next thing, in hopes that that will bring happiness and fill the emptiness.

The goal is to find some internal place of peace. It is an unreasonable goal to expect to stop missing your parent or grieving at some level. The hallmark is one's ability to live one's life to the fullest satisfaction and enjoyment, alongside the grief and loss. As a psychologist with more than twenty-five years experience, I find that this is possible when you are able to acknowledge your pain, have support for it, and the encouragement to live your life to your fullest potential—as a way to honor your parent or any adult who has loved and supported you. A fulfilled life is one that is surrounded by achievements, enjoyment, and connectedness.

When our parents or surrogate parents are proud of us, the world is a good place. Even after a parent has died, we can have this acceptance and pride.

When we are proud and satisfied with ourselves, the world is a perfect place. Even in life, we can supply this peacefulness for ourselves.

Thanks for going on this journey with us.
Frances Wollman Baumgarten, PhD

Made in the USA
Charleston, SC
05 July 2015